Prisoner Writing Projects

Write To Heal, Start Over & Reconnect

Reverend Mike Wanner

Table Of Contents

Dedication

This book is dedicated to those who are in prison and trying to figure out their situation. The causes of the actions that created the reasons for incarceration may have you wondering what happened.

There could be a number of things that coincided into the events that brought you to where you are. Even people who grow up with the proverbial silver spoon in their mouth can find themselves walking a path that takes them down a path to trouble.

Growing up is not easy for anybody and there is emotional adjustments needed as you mature. Lots of people do crazy things that they know they should not do and many of them get away with it because they do not get caught.

You may have anger at many kinds of authority as you grow up. Your parents, sibling, neighbors, teachers, ministers, rabbis, coaches, friends, teammates and many others may have let you down.

Unfortunately, you are the one in prison who is left holding the bag as the saying goes. Each day can be altogether different than the one before or you can stay upset with any injustices and be miserable.

You can choose to stay put or get moving again on your Life journey. This book will offer some ideas for your consideration.

1 - Why I am Writing This Book

I hope that this book continues the work started by my other books and continues to enhance the lives of Prison Employees, Prisoners, Taxpayers and the Families of Each of these groups?

As I have been writing these books on the subject of Prisons, the complexity of the process has been amazing to me.

The books that I have published so far about the prison situation are:

1. *Angel Raphael Speaks Volume 4: Angels, Addicts, Alcoholics & Prisoners – Oh Yeah!*
2. *Angel Raphael Speaks Volume 5:* Prisoners Caring for Alcoholics - Australia In Miniature Projects Intro
3. *Angel Raphael Speaks Volume 6:* Prisoners Caring for Addicts - Australia In Miniature For Addicts
4. *Prison Jobs Now: Providing Care For Addicts And   Alcoholics*
5. *Angel Raphael Speaks - Prisons* (A Kindle only book -2013)
6. *Contained Care Communities Concept*
7. *Australia In Miniature*
8. *Prison Possibilities Dialogue Series: Concept*
9. *Prison Possibilities Dialogue Series: Volume 2 Dialogues*
10. *Prison Possibilities Dialogue Series: Volume 3 Dialogues*
11. *Prison Possibilities Dialogue Series: Volume 4 Dialogues*
12. *Prison Possibilities Dialogue Series: Volume 5 Dialogues*
13. *Prison Possibilities Voluntary Exile: Concept*
14. *Prison Possibilities Correction Coaches: Concept*
15. *Prison Possibilities for Mexicans: Is A Boat Better than A Wall?*
16. *Prison Possibilities Family Time:* A Reason to Thrive!
17. Prison Genius Pool: "So Much Genius In Jail"
18. *Prison Possibilities Access Control: Prisoner Access by Request*
19. *Prisoner's Lawyers Can Save The American Economy: Make A Buck Doing It & Be Thanked!*
20. *Prisoner Family Talks, Days, Stays & Vacations: Connecting Helps Healing*

2 - Do You Know Why?

Do you know why you are in prison?
Are you blaming others?
Do you have any responsibility?

The culture we live in has a lot to do with why some folks find themselves in prison and do not know what they did, how they got there or what to do next. Culture is not the only culprit because communication can be a huge impediment to human interaction and emotional wellbeing.

The emotions of growing up in the world today can have a lot to do with a level of isolation that previous generations did not have. Electronic communications may be part of the reason for multiple perspectives because it has characteristics that may be more helpful in communicating under some circumstances and less helpful under other circumstances.

Communication in person has hearing, visual observation and the energetic connectedness of communicating with all happening at the same time. If someone is saying what you want to hear in person and you see them make a face as they do, you may understand that they do not really mean what they say and are only saying that because you want to hear it.

Communicating on the phone or text is not as full an interaction as an in-person conversation. Additionally, devices tend to make communication less of a bonding event. People at the same table can feel the demeanor of each other and avoid conflict by reading all the queues.

Generational communication is difficult enough as the priorities of the generations can be wildly different but then adding devices can add a whole level of complexity. Younger folks have normal inclination to be seen as their own adult person as early in life as possible and that may also compound communication issues and shorten the parental options for protecting their children from the proverbial big bad world.

Being seen as adult may be nice but It does not help when you have made a mistake and the judge rules against you. You would not want the judge to take anything for granted and there to be a result that you did not welcome.

You may now see that communication is important for your future. While communication with others is very important, the major part of communication for you in your current position is to be clear within yourself.

While you may have been able to take a lot for granted at your home with your family, you are not there now. Clear thinking, planning and communicating can help you to walk in freedom as soon as possible if possible.

I encourage you to be clear and get to work by understanding, healing, reconnecting, communicating and starting over.

3 - Where to Begin?

A lot of the underlying reasons for things that humans do is their emotional positioning about things in their life. Do you remember when you were happy in life? You can write a few lines about events when things changed or your age at the time of the change.

What?_____

Where?_____

When?_____

With Who?_____

How did You Feel Before?_____

_____

How did You Feel After?_____

_____

What triggered the event? _____

_____

Was there another way for you to handle this? _____

_____

Was the event you referenced, the cause for the actions that triggered your incarceration _____

_____

_____

4 - The Reality of Was, Is and Will Be

Chapter 3 was about what happened. So, you had what was and then that happened and now you are at a new point.

So, you are now at a point where you need to know what is going on and how you feel about it and what you can do about it. A part of you may only know how to function in the world of what was but you are no longer there.

You are in the here and the now at the present time at the present place and in the present circumstances. It may seems like I am over emphasizing this but the reality is that the skills that you need to deal with the here and now are the ones that you learned at an earlier time.

Those old skills and understandings may not work for you in the here and now. The sooner that you understand that and prepare yourself to open to a new array of skills will determine your ability to get on with the business of your life.

If you break a leg then you need to adjust to a slower path in the present day so that you can heal and get ready to do more later when you have more function, peace and patience.

So your job for now is to adjust to the pluses and minuses of where you are right now.

5 - Your Story Now

When you think about the way things are, you are also listening to what you think and then you may believe it. So, if you think the wrong thing about yourself, you can create a story and part of your life that is unreal.

You can change your story at any time so I encourage you to start the process as an optimistic observer of yourself,

What is the most important thing for you to focus on right Now? _____

What feeling will empower you?_____

Do you have negatives obstacles? _____

Are you willing to work out the negative?_____

Are you willing to sit and write your plan?_____

Will you invite God to help?_____

Will you schedule time in each week to start your story journal now? _____

Why Your Story Is Important

A house is built on a foundation and if the foundation is a mess then so will be the rest of the house. Your life is built on your foundation so you need to be sure it receives the support it needs from time to time. If it is not solid, get to work!

6 - Being Objective

It is difficult to objectively view your foundational story when you are actively inside it. There is great value in stopping the clock metaphorically and recording where you are to the best of your ability.

Your story now does not limit you in any way. It is like intersection signs that show you where you are. Staying at your story intersection can limit you so I do not recommend it.

If you get stuck in now and have no target destination, you can't go where you have not decided to go. Unfortunately, many people arrive at a story intersection and get stuck there for a considerable time.

Getting stuck is not limited to any particular group of people. Movie Stars are as vulnerable as military people, business executives, teachers and housewives and prisoners.

Imagine that all kinds of people in your prison community have emotional struggles from different sources and you may never know their story. Know that each of them may say something that can help you. If you listen, you can learn.

It would be nice if you could have your story on paper to edit without it being viewed by others. If you can put your story on paper, you can find a point of detachment where you might edit the words on paper first and then manifest the change in your life more easily.

7 - What Would Improve Your Story

Your story could be a detailed account of where you came from and what the situation is now. Include cultural references to your family ancestry, education, family business, religion, chronic family illnesses, marital status, etc.

As you review the list of items below, try to be aware of the emotions that come up and record them. Especially include feelings of heartache, betrayal, anger, fear and rage.

Consider if any of the following influence your old story:
Ancestry
Age
Living Locations
Education
Family culture
Family Business
Religious Upbringing
Family Illnesses
Marital Status
Military Service
Identified Traumas/Crimes
Racial Identity/Multiplicity
Medical History with Ages
Drug Dependency – Prescription
Drug Dependency – Street Drugs
Smoking
Alcohol Use
Family Crisis – Immediate Family
Family Crisis – Extended Family

8 - Get to Work on Your Story

Decide:

1. How will you keep your story?
2. How often will you work on it?
3. When will you start?
4. When will you finish it?

Step one - Get a notebook or start a computer page

Step Two – List influences from Chapter 7.

Step Three - Consider integrating the influences.

Step Four – Write out the truth of where you are including all the problems, opportunities, hurdles, challenges and your disappointments.

Step Five - Write a resolution of what three things you would like to change and which one of them is first, and second and third.

    a. First Resolution _____

    b. Second Resolution _____

    c. Third Resolution _____

9 - Where You Are Now

You have been dealt a hand in life. If you are not Royalty, You may not like it.

If you don't like it, Get real and Change the Deal. Drop the "'T" off "I can't" and make it "I can"

It's your life, you are in charge and you are the dealer. Shuffle the cards and begin to play within your own rules.

Now you say – "Can I change things?" That's simple: You change things by thinking about them differently.

Start walking on the path to Release. Acknowledge how you feel. Undo the lock that stress has on you by owning your feelings and asking for help. Who do you ask?

You may wish to say "God Help Me change."

You may not. Some people understand about God, whoever and whatever you believe God to be, and others just don't.

I believe that you can change things a lot easier with God's help but that is not for everyone so I cover many techniques on my website http://www.StressReleaseCoach.com.

You always have a choice in life even when it feels that you do not.

10 - Elimination of Limitations

Here is the technique for the Elimination of Limitations.

MAKE A LIST OF YOUR "I CANT'S" Spend some time on it. Try to be diligent and make sure you have them all.

Grade each with a priority code. Grade them A, B, C, D. A will equal the worst of the worst or you could say your best of the "I cant's" or you could say the things you absolutely can't do. Put them down on the list.

B will equal the next level of difficulty.

C will equal the next level of difficulty.

D will equal the least difficult things that you can't do.

Next, prioritize them in descending order from 10 (the worst) to 1 (the least) within their alphabetical grade. You would have A10 to A1, B10 to B1, C10 to C1, D10 to -D1.Yes you can have more that one of each but if you have a lot of one then you will need to further prioritize with sub-lists.

Print or write out the list in descending priority order.

Now that you have done all that work, give yourself a pat on the back because you are working at taking charge of your life and there are few more noble tasks. You are polishing the diamond that you are.

You are creating sparkle in your life, your family and your community. You are on your way to your power. Now get to work on this list.

Start with the Least D1. Get a pen or pencil (red if you have it) and take your D1 and make an x over the "'T" or get an eraser (Liquid or rubber) and remove the "'T". Make the remaining "I can" your affirmation for 3 days at least or as many as 21. "I can _____. " Say it at least three times a day, preferably a lot more. Take some action (one step minimum each day) towards the fulfillment of D1. Notice how it feels to do that.

Next, start with the worst. Get a pen or pencil (red if you have it) and take your A10 and make a red x over the "'T" or get an eraser (liquid or rubber) and remove the "'T". Make the remaining "I can" your affirma tion for 3 days at least or as many as 21. "I can _____. " Say it at least 3 times a day, preferably a lot more. Take some action (one step minimum each day) towards the fulfillment of A10. Notice how it feels to do that.

Take your next lowest and then your next highest. Etc.

WOW! After all that work, it is time to reward yourself. Remember to be gentle with yourself as you work to polish the diamond that you are.

11 - Do You Still Need Help?

Identify the leftover issues that you have not been able to get to the level that you want and then begin to work on them. Self - help circles for years have talked about the Pareto Principle which is sometimes referred to as the 80/20 rule.

The idea is that eighty percent of the benefits that you are able to receive from an effort is attained with the first 20% of your effort. After that, it will take the 80% of effort left to get the remaining 20% of the benefits.

Once you have the first 80% of benefits, it is time to be very selective of what you are putting effort to next. It is time to spend your effort wisely and find the people who can help you. Begin to decide what to realistically shoot for next and begin to

12 - Create A New Story

You can create for yourself a story of how you would like your life to be. Take every item from above and reset your priorities.

Develop and write the new story with your clearings and eliminations fully implemented. Establish the direction and processes you will travel and the destination for your goals.

Tell the tale of your power and manifestations as completely as you can envision. Put down every detail as vibrantly as you can.

You have done a lot if you are following my instructions. You have found out where you are and formed new thought patterns as to what you can do.

You have started the process of changing your thinking to align with a new reality that would be much more to your liking. You have created a vision of the path that will take you to the destination.

Congratulations. You are on your way.

As you go, challenges will surface and you get to reassess your priorities again and again. Some people may surrender and give up but that will not get you to a new peak on your trek to the top of the mountain of life.

Persistence can serve you well if you are consistently practical, diligent and disciplined as you set, evaluate and monitor your success on the path.

13 - Celebrate Your Progress

Accomplishing everything that we have talked about above has carried you very far forward on your path. It is important that you enjoy your success and really notice all that you have been able to accomplish.

It may be very tempting to push yourself further right away and try to fix everything about yourself in one fell swoop. This may not be the best idea because we all need time to adjust to new realities.

Please remember The Reality of Was, Is and Will Be. Take the time to adjust to the success that you have attained and pause to integrate it all in to the new story that you have just created.

Plan a date in the future when you will have had sufficient time to integrate your accomplishments. On that date, begin again to plan to polish the diamond that you are until it sparkles as bright as you desire it to.

Congratulations

Well Done

it

14 - Continuing On

While emotional pain was never an excuse for you or anybody to do what they wanted, realizing what you would like to do better can begin a new recognition of possibilities.

Emotional Pain may have kept you stuck for a long time and it could keep you stuck forever at a dead stop in your life. You could also file it in your emotional history instead of your current awareness.

Releasing painful events can help you to process the emotion of that time and put it in perspective. Choose well as you go forward and make up for past events that have blocked you.

You can find motivation by making up and making nice to release the damage to others and yourself as you move on with your life.

Compare life's mistakes to a wrong turn off the expressway. You could stop and do nothing or you can find out where you are, determine where you want to be and then work out a way to get from here to there.

Reading that may seem easy but it could have a big **BUT** in your view about changing it. Therein is the place to start.

When you have embraced the possibility for change, you can create that change. Congratulations again and again.

Life is never absolute. While breathing, you can change your mind, your body and your life.

Change starts on the inside and can happen in an instant. When you change your mind, you change your life.

15 - Clearing More Old Negative Energy

Some Things to Consider

Below I will list a bunch of titles for you to consider. If you feel any apply to you, make a note of it and what you want to do. When you are done, add any others that speak to you.

Next do what you decided to do so that you can clear the issue.

An Apology To God If You Feel It

_____

_____

_____

A Message To A Person You Wronged

_____

_____

_____

A Message To A Person Who Wronged You

_____

_____

_____

A Message To Each Child You Created

_____

_____

_____

A Message To Each Parent Who Created You

_____

_____

_____

A Message To A Parent That You Feel A Need To Say

_____

_____

_____

Declaration of Releasing An Old Story

_____

_____

_____

Claiming A New Story

_____

_____

_____

Planning Your Future Story

_____

_____

_____

A Message To Your Spouse

_____

_____

_____

Choose New Changes

_____

_____

_____

Message for God

_____

_____

_____

Prison Path to Real Power

_____

_____

_____

Prison Coaching Others to Success

_____

_____

_____

The Successful Rehabbed Prisoner

_____

_____

_____

Less Dense / Less Intense

_____

_____

_____

Success & Safety

_____

_____

_____

The Answers Can Come From Changing

_____

_____

_____

Choice Options

_____

_____

_____

Ideas For Taxpayer Savings

_____

_____

_____

Your Progress Plan

_____

_____

_____

The Prisoner Reality & Social Change Show

_____

_____

_____

For

Considering

These

Ideas

Ever

It Does Not Help

Prayer Still Does!

Resource http://www.Create-A-Prayer.com

18 - Resource List

Distant Healing Sessions (or Join Mail List) – Write To mikewann@voicenet.com
Books by Rev. Mike at www.Amazon.com

Veterans Healing Six Pack
1. *Trauma Healing Options for VA Hospitals: Help for Veterans to Own Their Healing and their future.*
2. *Trauma Healing Action Steps for Veterans: Help to Start Healing*
3. *Trauma Healing Action Steps for Veterans: Empowerment*
4. *Trauma Healing Action Steps for Veterans: Forgiveness*
5. *Trauma Healing Action Steps for Veterans: Thought Freedom*
6. *Tea For Veterans: Welcome One Home*

PTSD Power Pack:
1. *The PTSD Project: Turn Pain To Power*
2. *PTSD & Soul Retrieval: Putting One Back Together*
3. *PTSD & The Purple PAD: Calling all Scientists and PTSD Patients*

Angel Raphael Speaks Volume 1: Take Courage! God Has Healing in Store for You!
Angel Raphael Speaks Volume 2: Take Courage! God Has Healing in Store for You!
Angel Raphael Speaks Volume 3: Take Courage! God Has Healing in Store for You!
Angel Raphael Speaks Volume 4: Angels, Addicts, Alcoholics & Prisoners – Oh Yeah!
Angel Raphael Speaks Volume 5: Prisoners Caring for Alcoholics - Australia In Miniature Projects Intro
Angel Raphael Speaks Volume 6: Prisoners Caring for Addicts - Australia In Miniature For Addicts
Reiki Journaling from Japan
Reiki Is Alive: God's Great Gift
Four Parts to Healing
Distant Healing: We Are All Connected
Stress Release Energy Work: How To Cope
Does Reiki Love Heal Cancer?
Group Consciousness
Salute To Philadelphia VA Medical Center: Thank You
Reiki Transcript for Reiki 2 & 3 Channels: Dr. Usui Is That You?
God Bless Kindle & Amazon
Puppies Are Different From People
If Your Dog Dies
Toy Guns Are Obsolete

Great Spirit Made Children With Red Skin: AND
The Cage of Fear: Is Not Locked
God Made Children Red, Yellow, Brown, Black & White: Greet Each Child With Kindness
Emergency Medical Kindness In The Cradle Of Liberty: Big City - Cracked Bell
Angels Are Always Around Addicts and Addicts: Help Is Near Now! Invite It In!
Angels Are Always Around Addicts and Alcoholics: Volume 2 - Tools To Help Re-Light Your Life
Prison Jobs Now: Providing Care For Addicts And Addicts
Controlled Care Communities Concept
Prison Possibilities Dialogue Series: Concept
Prison Possibilities Dialogue Series: Volume 2, 3, 4, 5 Dialogues
Prison Possibilities Voluntary Exile
Prison Possibilities Corrections Coaches
Prison Possibilities For Mexicans: Is A Boat Better Than A Wall?
Prison Possibilities Family Time: A Reason to Thrive!
Prison Genius Pool: "So Much Genius In Jail"
Prison Possibilities Access Control: Prisoner Access by Request
Prisoner's Lawyers Can Save The American Economy: Make A Buck Doing It & Be Thanked!
Prisoner Family Talks, Days, Stays & Vacations: Connecting Helps Healing

Little Books at Kindle.com by Rev. Mike:
English Medical History Questionnaire For Non-English Speakers
English Language Helper For Non-English Speakers
Wise Wonderful Women Are The Well Of The Family
Answers for Test & Research: Dowsing Power
Crisis? Reiki! Baby? Reiki!
Bible References For Healing
Angel Raphael Speaks – Prisons
Angel Raphael Speaks – Veterans
The Saint Off Interstate 95

Angel Raphael Speaks through Rev. Mike Wanner. Please visit
http://www.AngelRaphaelSpeaks.com

19 - Angels Please Prayers

Addict's
Angels of Healing Selected
Help Me to Stay Directed
Come To Me From The Sky
I Am Ready to Succeed Not Try
If I Don't Invite You In
I Might Not Win
I Have Been Lost For Too Long
Help Me To Stay Strong

Alcoholic's
Angels of Healing On High
Help Me to Stay Dry
Come To Me From The Sky
I Am Ready to Succeed Not Try
If I Don't Invite You In
I Might Not Win
I Have Been Lost For Too Long
Help Me To Stay Strong

From

http://AngelRaphaelSpeaks.com/AAAAAAA/

20 - Private Channeling

Angel Raphael Speaks is a series of free messages that are channeled through Reverend Mike Wanner for the Highest good and Highest Healing of all concerned.

Many questions arise about Reverend Mike doing private channeling and he does help with that so e-mail him.

Reverend Mike is available world-wide as a psychic channel, emotional release facilitator, spiritual energy practitioner & teacher, and public speaker. He looks forward to meeting you soon!

Email - mikewann@voicenet.com 215-342-1270 PRIVATE SPIRITUAL READINGS/channelings or Spiritual Healing Sessions: Telephone or in person. Rev. Mike is available for private, one-on-one intuitive sessions with you, his Guide Family, and your Guides. He helps by offering clarity on emotional situations about your life, your purpose, your spirituality, and the release of stuffed emotions and cellular memory.

Connect to the love of your Guides today!
Contact Rev. Mike for an appointment.
Sessions available:

Spiritual Readings
Angel Channeling
Distant Reiki Healing
Distant Clearing of Stuffed Emotions
Distant Clearing Cellular Memory
Distant Clearing Energy Blockages
Distant Clearing of the Chakras
Customized needs
Mastermind dowsing responses to yes/no direction finding questions.

Rev. Mike is a facilitator of healing. He brings you and the Divine together so that you can align with the Divine and have a great time and a great life. All healing is between you and God, as it should be. Go ahead and start without Rev. Mike. Visit his prayer site http://www.Create-A-Prayer.com. Take the first step NOW.

21 - Reverend Mike Wanner

Rev. Mike Wanner started his metaphysical and ministerial studies with Reiki in 1993 and has studied seven styles of Reiki in the U.S., Japan, Canada, Denmark and Australia. He is certified to teach. He became certified to teach Integrated Energy Therapy in 1999 and co-taught the first IET class of the new Millennium. Mike began dowsing in 2001.

Ordained as a Metaphysical Minister of the International Metaphysical Ministry and an Interfaith Minister of the Circle of Miracles Ministry, Rev. Mike practices and teaches spiritual energy therapies in the Philadelphia Area.

Rev. Mike holds ministerial degrees from the University of Metaphysics and the University of Sedona. He is a Pastoral Care Associate of Aria - Frankford Hospital. He taught at the National Academy of Massage Therapy and Health Sciences.

Rev. Mike was a faculty member of the Medical Mission Sister's Center for Human Integration's School of Integrated Body/Mind Therapies in Fox Chase, Philadelphia, PA for twelve years.

Rev. Mike is licensed by the teaching of Intuitional Metaphysics to practice Spiritual Healing and Scientific Prayer. Mike is also a Prayer therapist.

Rev. Mike was elected in 2007 to the status of "Fellow of the American Institute of Stress."
In 2008, Rev. Mike became a practitioner of Coincidental Recognition as he incorporated the CoRe System in to his spiritual healing practice.

In 2009, Rev. Mike trademarked a new healing process called Quantum Quatro! Subtle Energy System Support®.

In 2011, Rev. Mike joined the outreach program known as the Health Advantage Group.

In 2012, Rev. Mike became a Certified Professional Coach by The Master Coaching Academy and Joined the Personal Empowerment Group.

Prior to his metaphysical, ministerial and coaching studies, Rev. Mike worked for Sears Roebuck and Co. while in High School and after graduation until he joined the U. S. Air Force in 1965. He returned to Sears from Vietnam in 1969 and stayed until 1978. His final Sears assignment was as an efficiency expert in Methods - Operational Research and Development.

He volunteered with Burholme Emergency Medical Services from 1969 and is still a Life Member and Board of Directors Member. He started a private ambulance company in 1975 and worked professionally in the field until 2001 when he devoted his full attention to real estate investing, healing, coaching and writing.

www.ReverendMikeWanner.com

www.ingramcontent.com/pod-product-compliance
Lightning Source LLC
Chambersburg PA
CBHW061236180526
45170CB00003B/1320